WALK Berlin
Photo Travel Guides

Tyler Barnard

Analog Design Studio

Analog Design Studio
www.analogdesignstudio.com

WALK™ Berlin
Photo Travel Guides

Copyright © Analog Design Studio, LLC. 2008 All rights reserved. This material may not be reproduced, displayed, modified or distributed without the express prior written permission of the copyright holder. For permission, contact www.analogdesignstudio.com or 303-835-3564.

ISBN 978-0-615-20400-0

More **WALK**™ Travel Guides can be found at:
www.walktravelguides.com

Disclaimer: We have made every effort to locate and verify the original location and author of the photography in WALK Berlin. If you find an error in location or feel that your copyrights have been abused please contact us at photos@walktravelguides.com and we will address the issue as soon as possible. Some of the information in this book such as e-mail addresses and photographer locations are subject to change. The publisher cannot be liable for such discrepancies over time. We, the publishers make no suggestion of where, how, when or why you should travel, therefore we cannot be liable for your travels based upon the use of this book. We value your feedback, suggestions and comments. Please contact us at info@walktravelguides.com.

Introduction

To all the travelers who seek to find themselves in something unknown.

The idea for a series of photographic travel books came from a desire to give travelers a break from the endless pages of descriptive text. Instead, we have chosen to visually represent each city as a collection of daily experiences. Through our visual tour, our photographs take into account the people, architecture, history, culture and more. Our hope is to capture the essence of each place so that you, the audience, can gain an understanding of what a place might be like. This is not an ordinary guidebook, becaues in **WALK**™Travel Guides the journey is completely left up to you. We do not endorse restaurants, hotels, or even a given itinerary. We simply excite you about the possibilities of travel. So whether you are a seasoned traveler or just embarking on your first adventure, we invite you to take us with you along the way.

~the **WALK**™travel team

Content

06   Map: Berlin Center

08   Pankow: Prenzlauer Berg

26   Mitte: Central Berlin

46   Friedrichshain-Kreuzberg

62   Mitte: Tiergarten & Wedding

84   Charlottensburg & Wilmersdorf

98   Acknowledgements

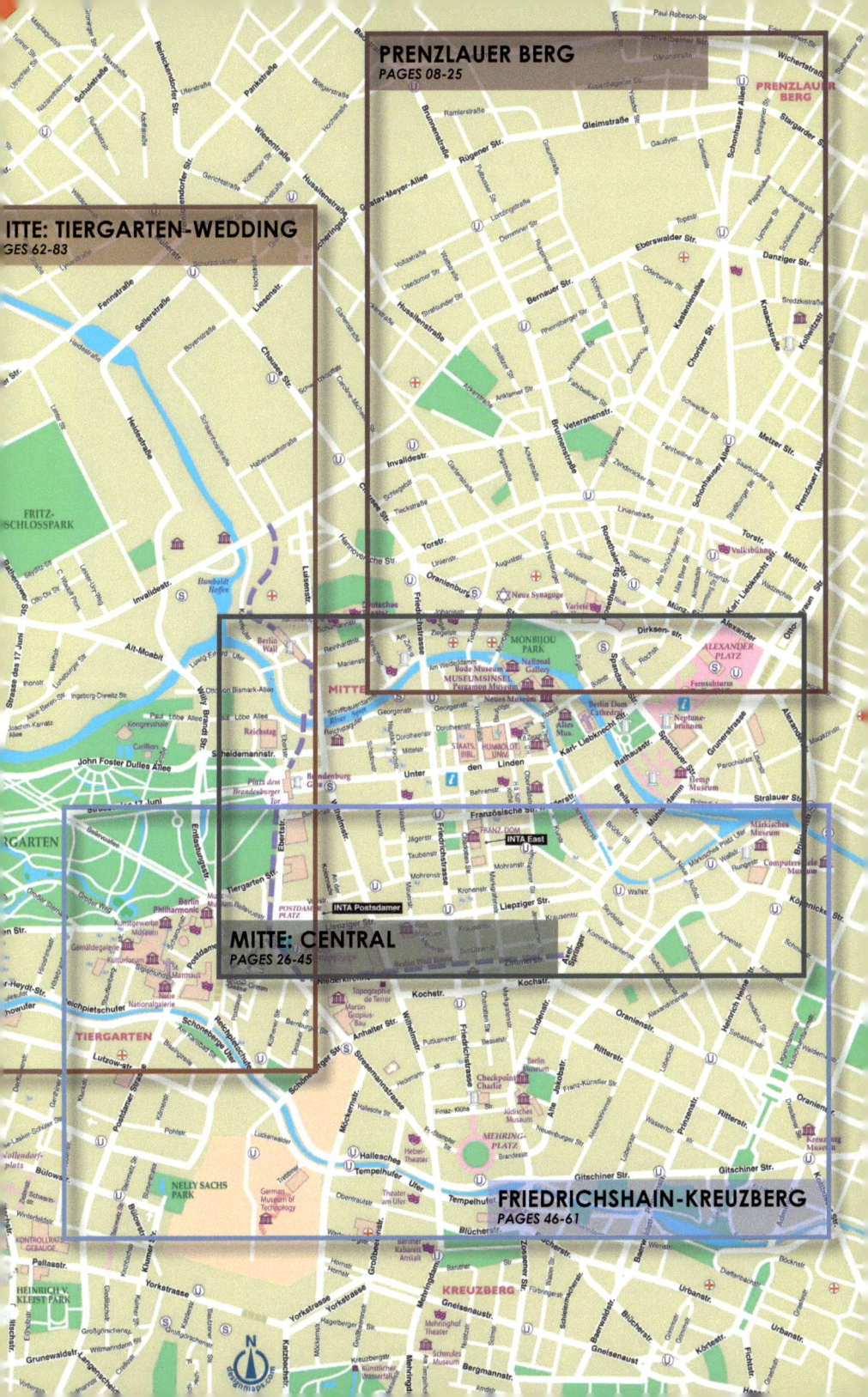

PRENZLAUER BERG

www.walktravelguides.com

Prenzlauer Berg | Berlin By Boroughs

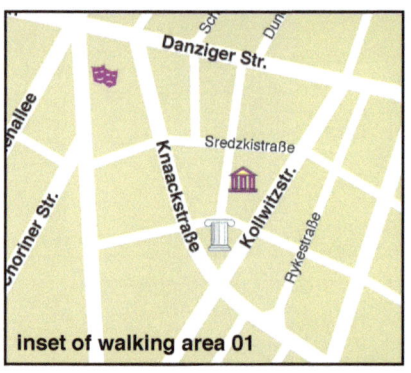

inset of walking area 01

www.walktravelguides.com

Prenzlauer Berg | Berlin By Boroughs

inset of walking area 01

www.walktravelguides.com

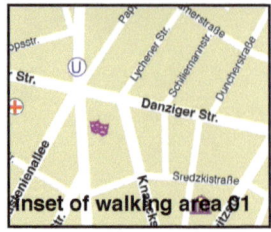

Inset of walking area 01

www.walktravelguides.com

Prenzlauer Berg | Berlin By Boroughs

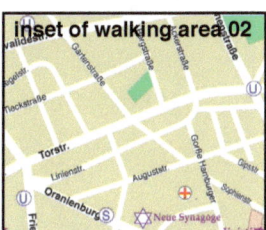

www.walktravelguides.com

inset of walking area 02

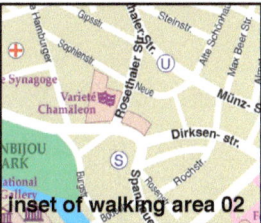

inset of walking area 02

24 Prenzlauer Berg | Berlin By Boroughs

inset of walking area 02

www.walktravelguides.com

MITTE: CENTRAL

Walking Area 02
pg 38-45

INTA Postdamer

Berlin Friedrichstraße

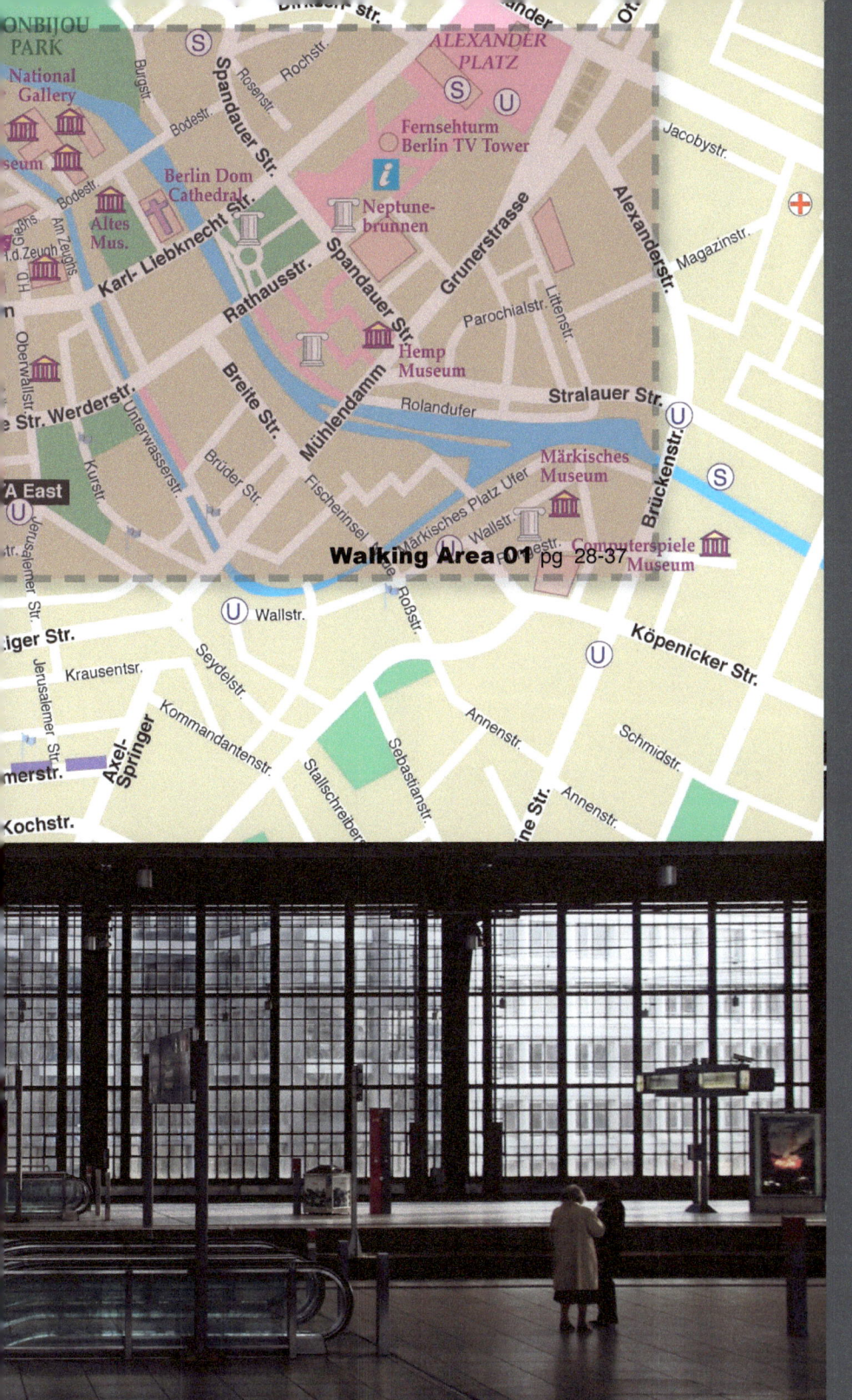

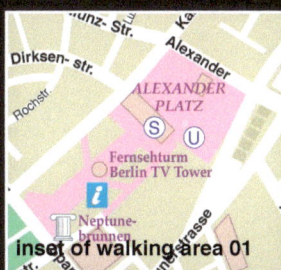
inset of walking area 01

Mitte: Central | Berlin By Boroughs 31

Inset of walking area 01

www.walktravelguides.com

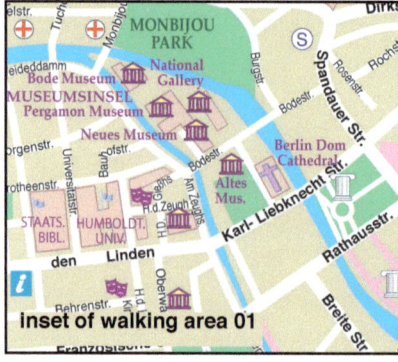

inset of walking area 01

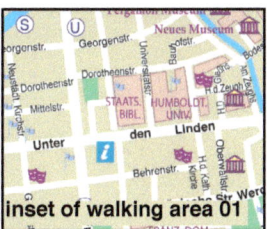

inset of walking area 01

www.walktravelguides.com

Mitte: Central | Berlin By Boroughs

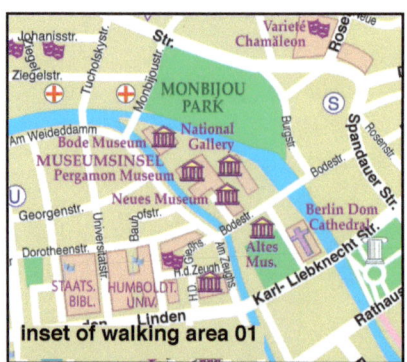

Mitte: Central | Berlin By Boroughs

inset of walking area 02

www.walktravelguides.com

Mitte: Central | Berlin By Boroughs   43

inset of walking area 02

www.walktravelguides.com

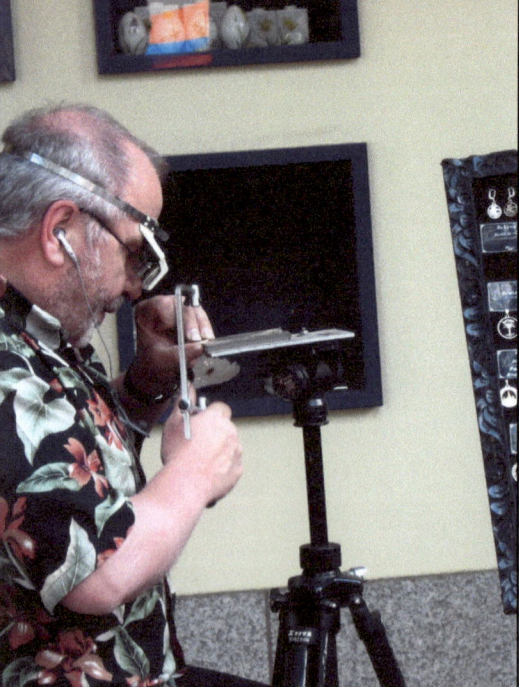

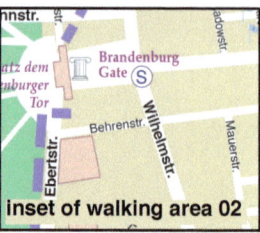

inset of walking area 02

www.walktravelguides.com

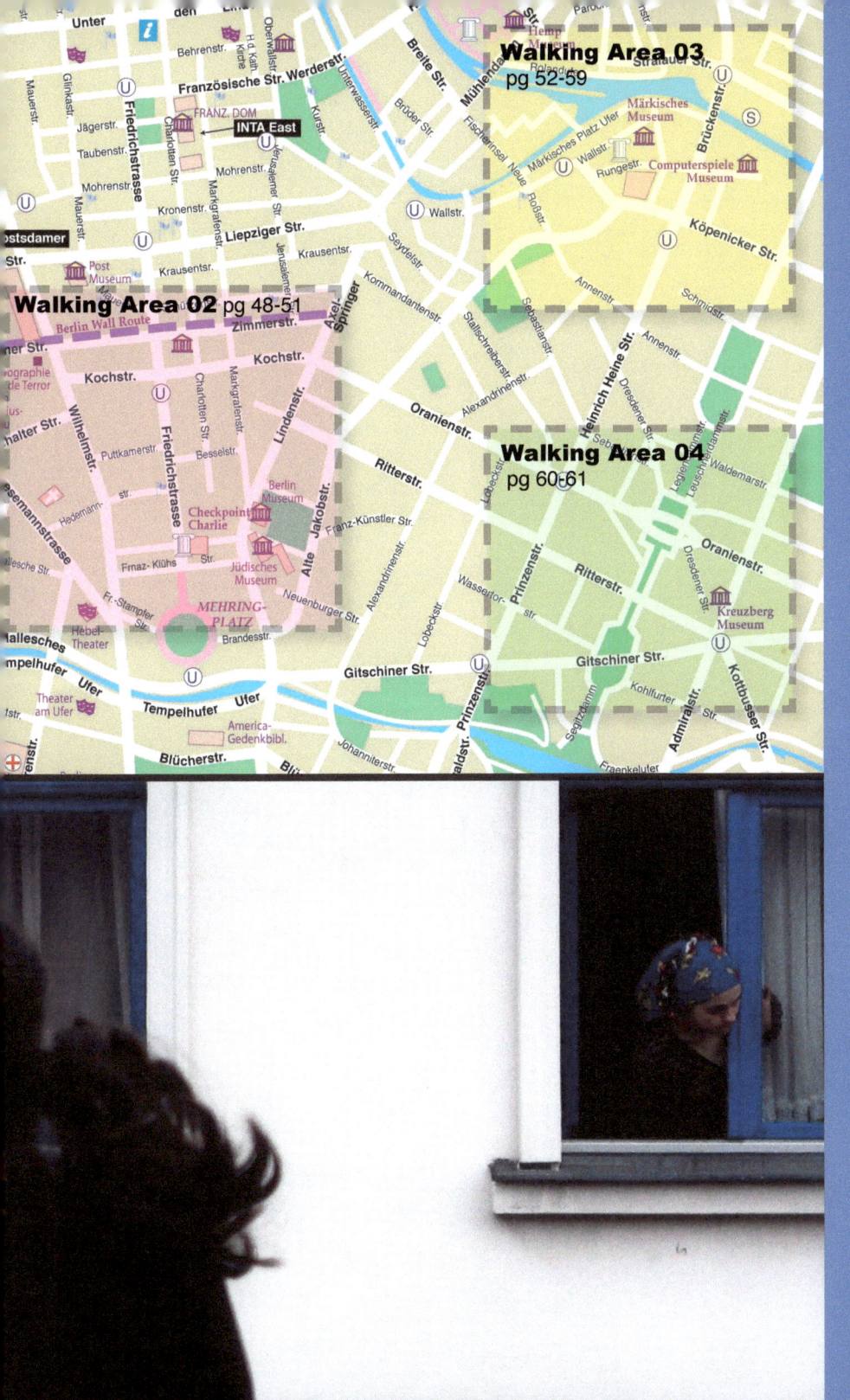

Friedrichshain-Kreuzberg | Berlin By Boroughs

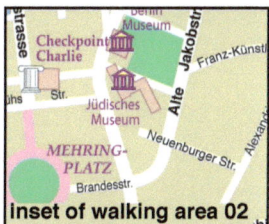

inset of walking area 02

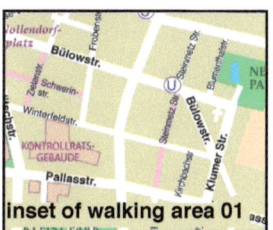

inset of walking area 01

inset of walking area 02

Friedrichshain-Kreuzberg | Berlin By Boroughs

inset of walking area 03

www.walktravelguides.com

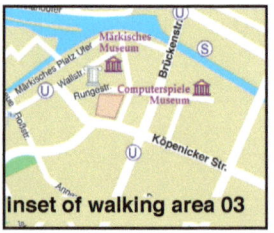

Inset of walking area 03

www.walktravelguides.com

inset of walking area 03

inset of walking area 03

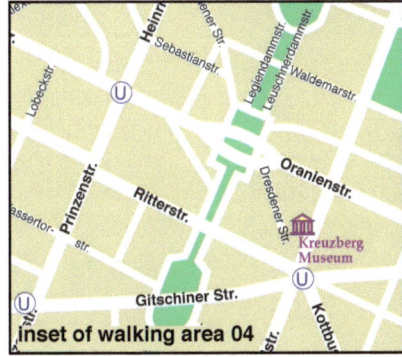

inset of walking area 04

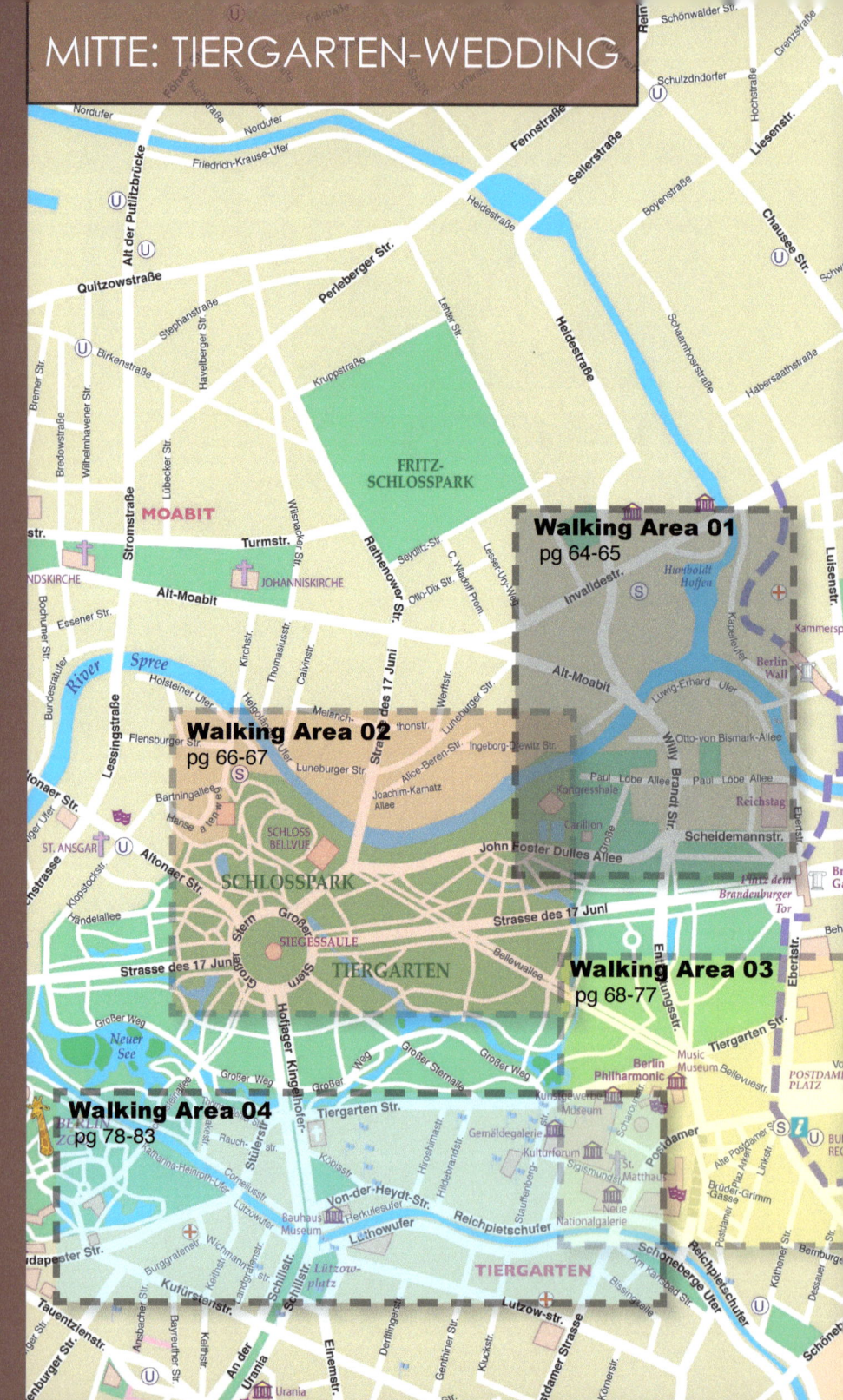

inset of walking area 04

www.walktravelguides.com

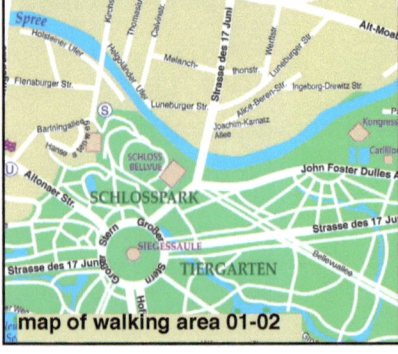

map of walking area 01-02

www.walktravelguides.com

Mitte: Tiergarten-Wedding | Berlin By Boroughs

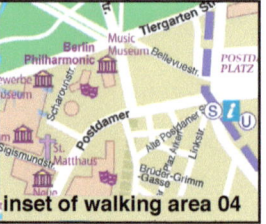

inset of walking area 04

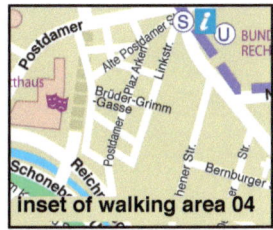

inset of walking area 04

www.walktravelguides.com

inset of walking area 04

Mitte: Tiergarten-Wedding | Berlin By Boroughs

inset of walking area 04

78 | Mitte: Tiergarten-Wedding | Berlin By Boroughs

inset of walking area 04

www.walktravelguides.com

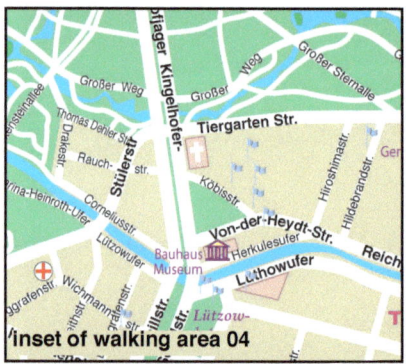

Inset of walking area 04

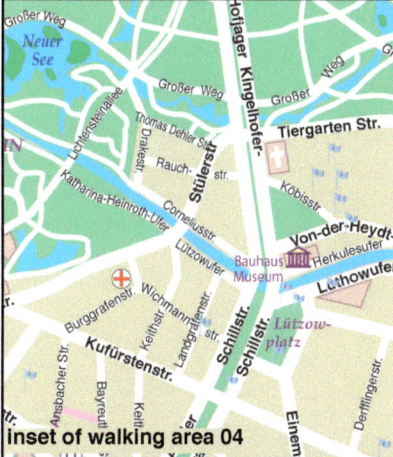
inset of walking area 04

CHARLOTTENSBERG-WILMERSDORF

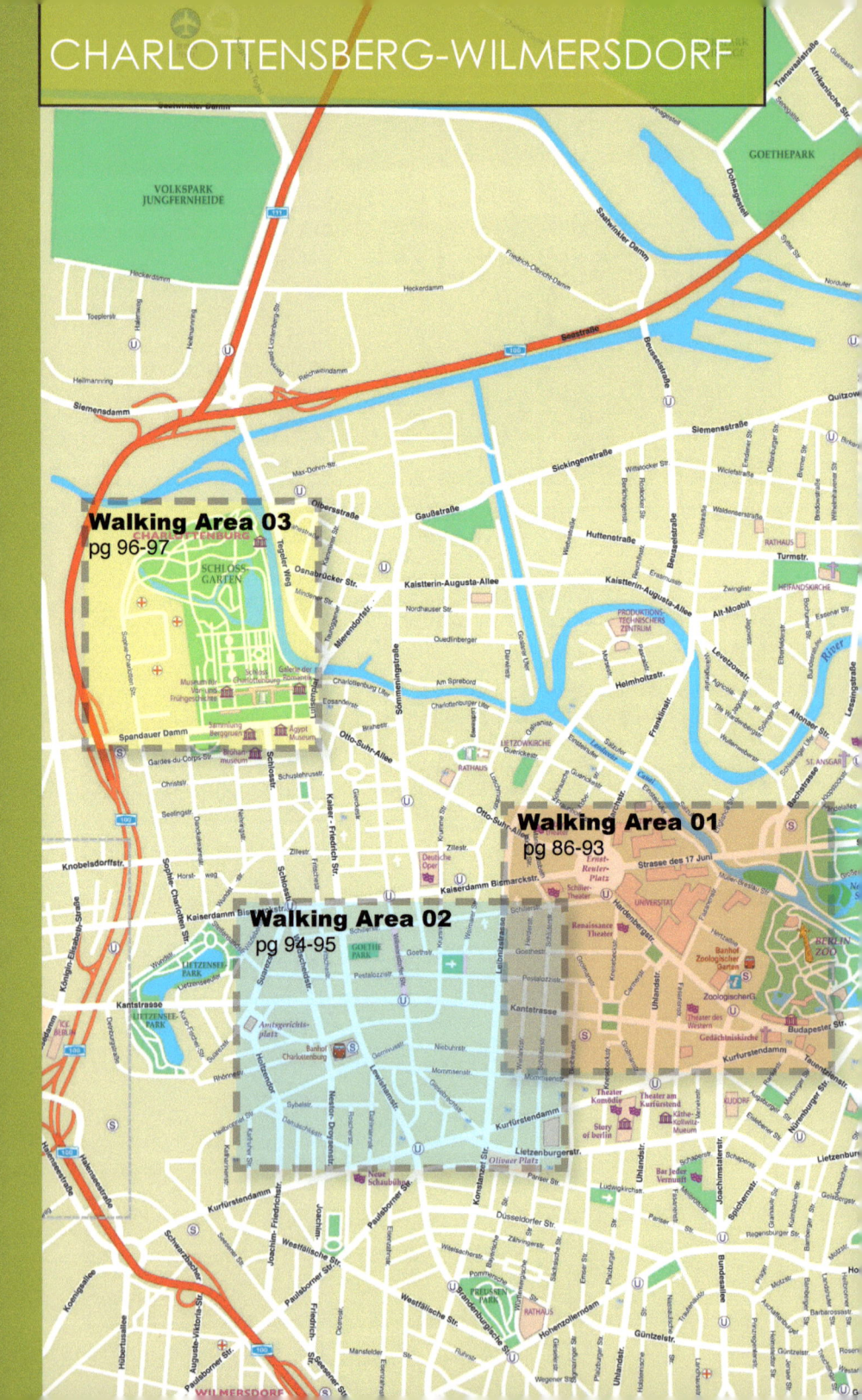

www.walktravelguides.com

Charlottensburg-Wilmersdorf | Berlin By Boroughs

inset of walking area 01

www.walktravelguides.com

Charlottensburg-Wilmersdorf | Berlin By Boroughs

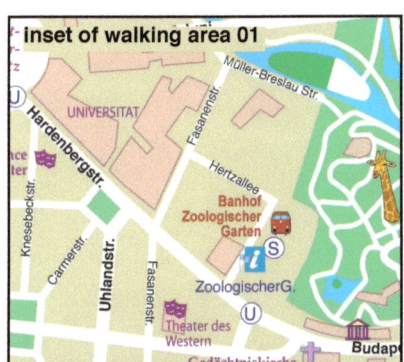

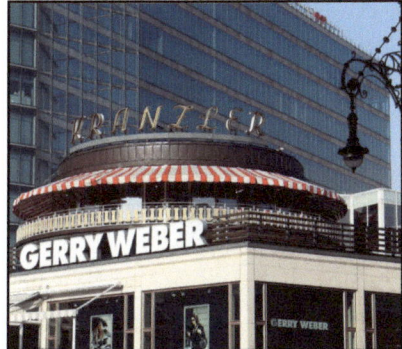

inset of walking area 01

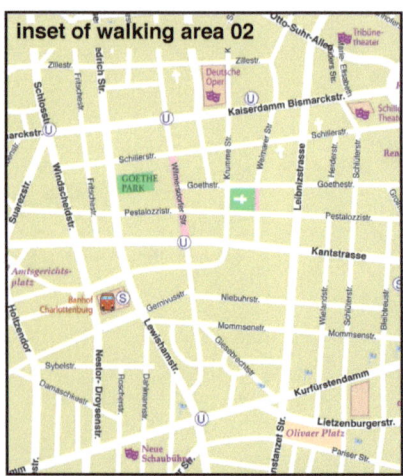

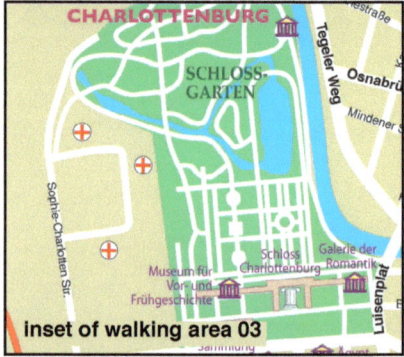

www.walktravelguides.com

The Author | Lead Photographer
Architect and Photographer Tyler Barnard combined his passions for design and traveling to create the WALK™ Travel Guide series. You can learn more about his journeys at www.tylerbarnard.com

For Analog Design Studio, LLC:
Publishing Director
Tyler Barnard

Editor
Lauren Sabel

Design & Layout
Tyler Barnard

Cartography
Scott Lockheed
www.designmaps.com

Additional Photographers:
Flickr Photo Contest Winners

Listed in alphabetic order: Erin Ball; Gregoire Cachemaille; Alberto Girón Castillo; Lorenzo Conte; José Antonio Salinas Fernández; Sabine Fink; Martina Foschini; Leonidas Halkidis; Trevor Hart; Gabriele Helfert; Dirk Jensen; James Jessiman; Thomas Lottermoser; Lauren Manning; Frank Nagel; Inga Opitz; Jaap Vogel; Sven Werkmeister
www.walktravelguides.com/contest

Picture Credits
Photographs in WALK™ Berlin are for sale on our website www.walktravelguides.com/

We would like to thank the contest winners for permission to reproduce their photographs. We would also like to congratulate them on winning the WALK™ Berlin Photo Contest. Enter your photos at www.walktravelguides.com/contest

Listed in alphabetic order:
Erin Ball - Hackescher Markt S-Bahn p23bl; Berliner Dom p32tl; St. George p32tr; Gendarmenmarkt p36cr; Entrance to the Bode Museum p43tr; Berlin Hauptbahnhof p65cbl; Symetry anyone? p96t; Schloss Charlottenburg p97 & 96cr. **Gregoire Cachemaille** - The London police p53bl; Untitled p54tr; Untitled p54trc; Hauptbahnhof p65tcl. **Alberto Girón Castillo** Untitled p35bl. **Lorenzo Conte** – appuntamento al billy wilder's p77c; traffic jam p77b. **José Antonio Salinas Fernández** - Sein und Zeit p28cl; Traveling in the Spree p31cr; Spielen vor dem Reichstag p40t; Through the window. Opposite directions p46-47b; Fireman fantasy p52; Desplazamiento p53t; Crossing the bridge p53cr; Bundeskanzleramt p65cbl; Ready to fly p67; The power of art p78tl. **Sabine Fink** - Untitled p40cl; Untitled p77tl; Untitled p80tl; Untitled p87; Untitled p91cl. **Martina Foschini** - Berlin Door p95; Jugendstil p94b. **Leonidas Halkidis** - Untitled p35cr; Untitled p94tr. **Trevor Hart** - Checkpoint Charlie p51; Statue inside the Potdamer Platz shopping mall p63; Schloss Charlottenburg p96b. **Gabriele Helfert** - Tacheles p20b; Hackesche Höfe p23tr; Bahnhof Friedrichstrasse p26-27b; HackescheHöfe p23tl; Alexanderplatz p29; Three in Berlin p35tr; Gendarmenmarkt p37; Pretty in Pink p38; Museum für Kommunikation p43tl; Chocolate Paradise p43bl; Neo-baroque p43cr; Brandenburger Tor p44cr; Close to Checkpoint Charlie p50c. **Dirk Jensen** - Alex p28b; Potdammer Platz p76. **James Jessiman** - Untitled p45. **Thomas Lottermoser** - Currywurst p54bl. **Lauren Manning** - Unter den Linden in the snow p42; DZ Bank p44tr; East Side Gallery p57tl; Neue Nationalgalerie p78cr. *continued next*

Frank Nagel - Bebelplatz p36cl. **Inga Opitz** - The shadow p28cr; Der Brezelkurier p30; Der Flaneur p33; Berlinszene p36b; Looking through an airshaft p50tl; Trabi-Tourismus p50b; Show me your real face p53br; Abend p55; Der Spaziergang p54ctr; Am Landwehrkanal p54cbr; Spree and Abend p56; Playing ball p59; 34 p58c; Urbanes Labyrinth p64; Giganten p65tl; Strandbar p65bl; Bundeskanzleramt p65ctr; Schloss Bellevue p66c; Haus der Kulturen der Welt p66tr; Artificial landscape p73tr; Museumsbesuch p79; Waves of concrete p82. **Jaap Vogel** - Berliner Dom p32c; Marie-Elisabeth-Lüders-Haus p39b. **Sven Werkmeister** - Dark Rider p32br; Gendarmenmarkt p36tr; Colors p54tl; Bicycles p68; Bahnhof p69c; Tower p70bl; Clouds p70cr.

tl-top left; tr-top right; cl-center left; cr-center right; bl-bottom left; br-bottom right

All other photographs: wCopyright © Analog Design Studio, LLC. 2008 All rights reserved.

Bulk Purchases
For bulk purchases of 10 or more copies or for personalized copies please contact info@walktravelguides.com

WALK Berlin
Photo Travel Guides

published by

Analog Design Studio
303-835-3564
Please send us your feedback: info@walktravelguides.com

Photographer?
WALK™ Travel Guides and **Analog Design Studios** are always on the look out for Lead Photographers to spearhead one of our books. Visit **www.walktravelguides.com/photographers**

Purchase WALK™ **Photographs**
The photographs you see in **WALK**™ Travel Guides are for sale. You can purchase prints, framed photographs and more. Please Visit: **www.walktravelguides.com.**

Blogs, Travel Tips and Forums
Please visit our website for more information on your next destination. Our city blogs give you up-to-date travel experiences direct from our photographers. Log onto our forums and share your own experiences or check our travel tips. Visit **www.walktravelguides.com**

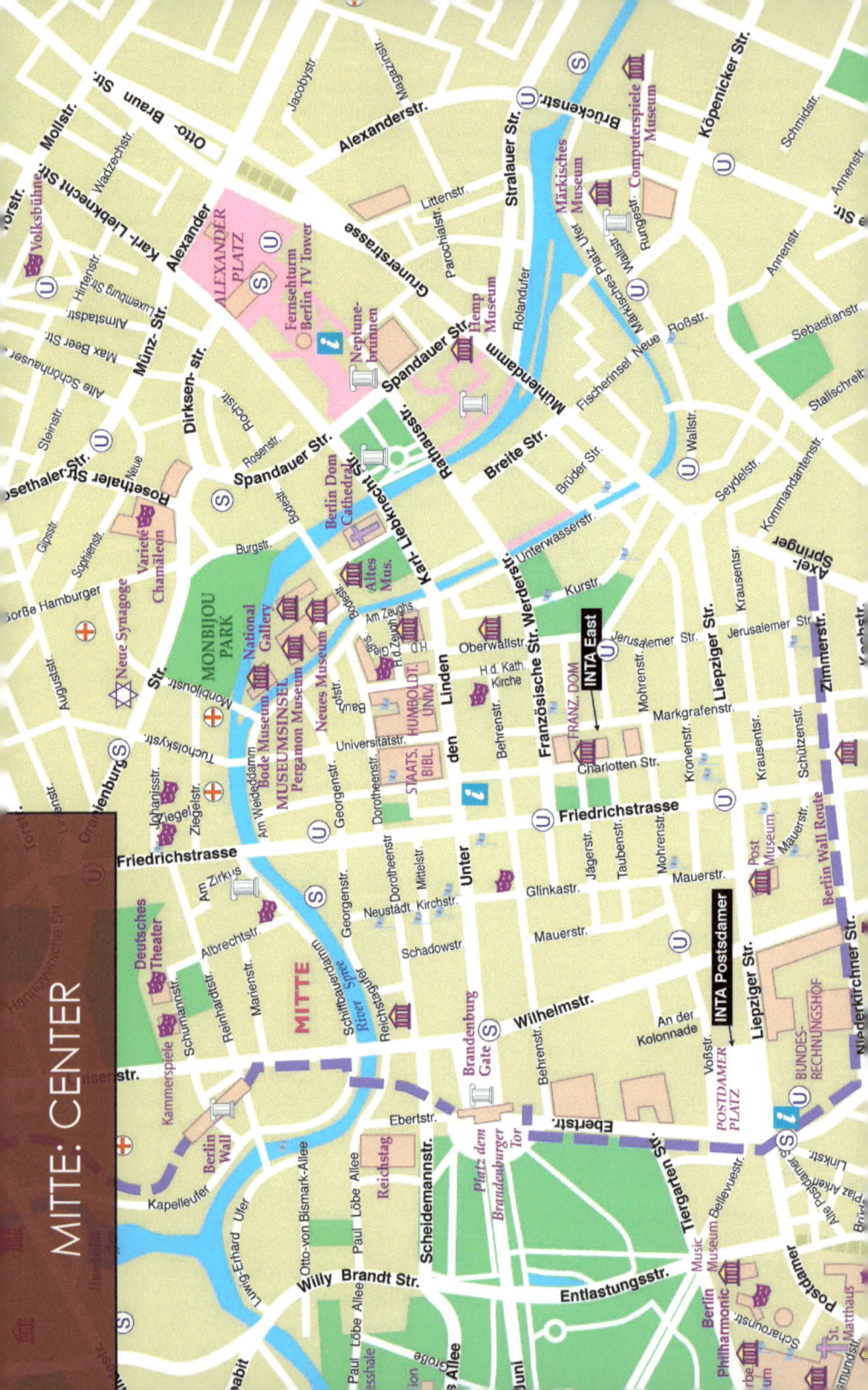

www.ingramcontent.com/pod-product-compliance
Lightning Source LLC
Chambersburg PA
CBHW042323150426
43192CB00001B/30